The Man Who Got Away

Also by New Academia Publishing

ALWAYS THE TRAINS: Poems, by Judy Neri

IN BLACK BEAR COUNTRY, by Maureen Waters

See inside the book at **www.newacademia.com** and read an excerpt.

The Man Who Got Away

Poems by Grace Cavalieri

Washington, DC

Library of Congress Control Number: 2014945059
ISBN 978-0-9904471-3-9 paperback (alk. paper)

 An imprint of New Academia Publishing

 New Academia Publishing
PO Box 27420, Washington, DC 20038-7420
info@newacademia.com - www.newacademia.com

"I have thee not/ but yet I see thee still—"

Hamlet

For Ken
1930—2013

*and to my daughters, grandchildren, and friends, who make me love
the only life I have*

Contents

Acknowledgments

Grateful thanks to the following magazines that have published some of the poems:

Poets&Artists; MiPOesias; Innisfreepoetryjournal; BeltwayPoetryQuarterly; Lummox; DoloresKendrick.com; danmurano.com; Truck; King's Estate Press; Paterson Literary Review; Dragonfly; fluent; Lips #42/43; King's Estate Press; ARLIJO.com; Loch Raven Review; iartistas.

And to the publishers of the following books and chapbooks from which poems have been extracted:

Bliss (Hillmunn Roberts Publishing House, 1986), *Trenton* (Belle Mead Press, 1990 &1992), *Cuffed Frays* (Argonne House Press, 1991), *Poems: New & Selected* (Vision Library, 1998), *Heart On A Leash* (Red Dragon Press, 1998), *Sit Down Says Love* (Argonne House Press, 1999), *This Sounds Like Something I Would Say* and *Navy Wife* (Casa Menendez, 2010), *Why I Cannot Take A Lover* (Washington Writers Publishing House, 1975) .

About the Book

This is a book of poems— more than a literary exercise— a document, testament, memorial for someone I met when I was 13 years old, and knew my entire life.

Ken Flynn and I were married almost 60 years when he left me.

Each poem is a note in a diary of loss. The words "dead" and "death" appear more than I would otherwise allow in my writing but honest emotions called these poems forth. In fact I have forgiven myself for many things so that I can make my feelings permanent.

Interspersed with poems of the present, are poems *about* Ken or *for* Ken from past books. I thread these throughout, and note on those reprinted poems books of origination. The past and present braided together make up my tribute. A small paper monument.

Grace Cavalieri

1952

There you sit in the open cockpit
I never saw such a smile
Goggles pushed up on your head
Shoulders harnessed with a parachute
To keep you safe
This would be before you were on 9 carriers
Before exile to Viet Nam
Before your children surrounded you like stars
Waiting for your kiss
Before the Autumns of our lives
Before there would be no Autumns
Before I said don't fly away
Before you would become someone else
Then back again
Before there would be so much sun outside without you
Before the winds were light and variable
Before you'd sit on the front step every time
I went to the store waiting for my return
There you are sitting in a cockpit of an SNJ
Smiling at me for all eternity
In a moment that could not last
Cleared for flight
Everything in the whole blue world
Ahead of you.

Going South

I love to think of it
Traveling south that time

Thirty years ago
Stopping

A sunlit town
A weekday afternoon

A town so small
Four corners with

Its children
Coming home from school

Green lawns, sweet air
Georgia or

Some other foreign place
Never seen before

No highways then
Bypassing

Sounds
Of people walking, talking

Three o'clock far away
My shoulders, a pink halter

No one dead
My mother, father, sister still alive

Nothing much to worry me
But the road

Ahead
Flowers, soft aromas

Strange trees
And a restaurant

I see just where we sat
That corner over there

The smell and feel of honey
But most of all warm sun

Beside a road
By a car headed south

Flavors of a southern town
Years ago, my first time down.

Bliss, 1986

One Year Ago Today

(January, 2014)

You came into the kitchen and I was making tea--- and you said
I feel a little debilitated today
You wore your warm grey sweatshirt
But your hands were shaking
And you said
I'll just take some cough medicine and go on back to bed
This was hours before the ambulance

Today, one year later, I feel a little debilitated myself
So I took some cough medicine and went back to bed
And dreamed you wanted to come Christmas shopping
You wanted to come with me to get yourself a gift
a Science kit for sculpting
As yours was empty
I had one bag left that we could use

I took my floppy hat and biked down the hill
And stopped to call you at McDonalds
But my phone was home with you
The nice Asian girl let me use hers but you didn't answer
So up the hill I went to tell you where we'd meet
And you were there!   You were here!

In your bright red sweater in my office in my chair
Today   Of all days
You always said that you knew how to thrill me
And you do   you do   you were there.

I Am Not Lazy. This Is One Thing I Am Not

I keep a tidy kitchen.
When irreparable damage had been done
I gave up smoking but for maybe just
One cigar a day. I emptied all the trays.
When news reached us of the undue
Hardships I divided the wind as
A factor, the speed as a factor
And puffed up the pillows in the next room.
When armies of enemies and friends advanced
Unlimited, I saw someone who looked
Like your wife and bought a
Picture of her for you to put on your desk.
When bullets hit dead center I said
What is the use of all the people we
Did not love and who did not love us.
I put them out with the garbage.
Before we killed an animal for
Supper we begged his pardon on
Our knees like Cherokees.
When strong currents ripped away
The walls I claimed it was the
Only way to stop the runaway cars.
Tasting the air like snakes without
Noses we've crawled along a long time
Finding our directions.
That's why I can honestly say I am

And have always been a good if not excellent
Housekeeper.

Why I Cannot Take A Lover, 1975

Garden Party

This isn't so bad I said. Everything's the same. You're just not here. Look.
I get up and make tea and you're just not here, that's all. I go swimming.
I shop and I can carry groceries in with just one hand now. I can keep
the house tidy and I don't have to cook. I watch movies. This is the life.
Then I called you at four for tea. And you didn't answer. No matter how
many times, you still didn't. Then the cat grew into a dog with pink eyes
and shaggy matted fur, the grass already sodden with rain was watered
all night with the hose. The people who came talked about the wrong
books. I couldn't make them understand it was the young librarian not
the movie critic. You said you'd take the cat to the vet, you said you
didn't care what it cost, you'd put new sod down, you said you'd make
everyone understand what I was trying to say. I kept calling and calling
because I know the dead have memory. I know you remember my name.
Everyone is here waiting.

Tarot Card VI. The Lovers

Having loved me when I was young
and now when I am not,
you are twice blessed
for giving
a rich person a gift.

In no one else's dream but yours,
I will be the old lady
wearing a white straw hat
with a red satin bow
who says   Thank you.

Sit Down, Says Love, 1996

Looking at the Sight of His Back

I am sorry for your loss   Please Accept   My condolences for your loss
Our sympathies   I am sorry   Accept my condolences   So sorry truly
My condolences for your loss   Our sympathies for your loss   Please

We rise to tea and homemade bread,
talk of a friend and read a prayer,
go swimming, nap, take a
machine to the fixer, cook pasta
in clam sauce, we drink vodka
martinis, how we complain about
our last house guest, we light a fire
in the fireplace, eat dinner
read a book, the day
slips beneath our surface,
how long were the shadows
tucked into the sly folds of our
marriage, we kept looking at the
sky trying to make sense of it,
no one else could do that for us,
those who loved us and left
no longer mattered. If we stop telling this story
it will go away.

What I Won

The sack dress was in style then
     with a single strand of pearls.
The sack dress was designed to see
     the body move lightly beneath.
That's why I wore it to my first poetry
     contest in Philly,
leaving my four-month-old at home.
     Of course my husband had to
drive, as nervous as I was
     so he waited in the car all
day while I sat in the big room, first time out
     since I found my mother
dead and then had a baby two weeks later.
     My husband stayed all day in that
car in the snow. I won first prize about
     wanting my mother but
It was said much better than this,
     as you can imagine, to win first.
It even began with *notes upon a phantom*
     lute, although The Poet
said what do we know of lutes now?
     But what did he know of
walking into her bedroom and finding
     her a pale shade of lilac.

That just goes to prove I guess I was talking
        about the wrong thing in the poem,
and The Poet was surely on to something.
        I have to say I looked wonderful,
gaunt with grief and colitis, 1956,
        hurrying across the street
where my husband was waiting to take me home,
        the first wrong victory in my hand.

Sounds Like Something I Would Say, 2010

The Corner Street Café

Last night my husband and I had to cancel our performance.

We'd been practicing it for years.

The script—

Our parts—

We even carried firewood up the stairs. All the props were there.

The audience was small, as usual, at the Corner Street Café

But our loyal friends were waiting for us when we walked in.

I announced that we were cancelling the play tonight and, of course

Apologized for inconvenience.

Some were relieved with important planes to catch. Others,

Like the Director, were a little more insistent. "Just give a reading,

Say a poem, do something, anything. They all came here for you."

I looked at the sorry script in my hand held together through the years

Stapled, bent and smeared.

I couldn't put the actors through that, I thought.

I then said that line aloud and the audience cheered.

"Read a poem," my husband said, since everyone is seated.

I did. Then a brave young woman in a purple knit blouse stood,

"I applaud you for not putting this on.

It is so cruel to the characters in the script,

depicting them with such pain and loss."

This was turning out to be a Q & A without a play,

"Why did you cancel something so well-rehearsed for so many years?"

We forgot the technical part, I admitted. We never brought the audio.

My husband and I are still together, I explained, and will be forever.
But without his life support equipment there's no communication.
He just cannot be heard.

Three Days in a Row

Three days in a row without a bad dream,
your luck must be changing, that's why I wanted you to
identify the strange bird outside, the one
with the call. Yet
it was beyond the hearing of
your ear once filled with so many jet planes
resting now in an ocean of quiet.
I can't know these things alone,
I said, It's like language
sleeping, no one else can hear.
No! I can't have it. It's bad enough that death will happen
but the bird is here now
and so are we. It's not fair to me, or the birds, for that matter,
You lifted your chin, tilting your head slightly:
It's a song sparrow, you said, moving in nearer. *I'm sure it's a sparrow.*

Cuffed Frays, 2001

I'll Take That as a Compliment

Dancing in the basement of the Pentagon
every Friday night –they'd open up for
disco lessons and how we'd been waiting
to learn those steps. Elaine the accountant in
my office would come with her new boyfriend
although his little kids vomited on her
their first time at the picnic,
but maybe Elaine could make it after all to
this kind of carefree bouncing fast music.
Her ex-husband locked her out and kept the
family punch bowl, and Ken and I were badly
in need to find something new in our marriage.
This just might be it, finding the moves to
Donna Summer urging us on. Oh yes, they
pushed the desks aside to clear the space
for continuing education in the Pentagon
basement for people like us, except the
only trouble is we both wanted to lead. We
learned the grapevine and the side wind and
outlasted Elaine and Ted, but every week
we found we needed to start all over again.
Maybe if we had a strobe light, my husband
said, *I'm willing to. Are you?*

The Return

From the white winters
from the stone letters
after guarding the night
the end of our differences
from the colonized heart
the mournful moral lessons
into the electronic age
the versions of ourselves
in the breeze from the waters
hoarding its memories

Navy Wife, 2010

Glass Metal Salt

Your hands on my neck so transparent
I could see through them in my sleep,
as I move into the city of windows lying at my feet.
I am the only 3rd dimension
on a flat map world—

My Monk in the machine! Talk to me. Anything,
Tell me how it breathes for you, pumping
against your will. Tell me how you love heavy metal,
my pilot, my race car driver, my sculptor,
how you want to get your hands on it, make it move,

fly, shape and burnish it. I see you know—it's winning—
This is the one thing you cannot bend,
but if I know you, and I do — you'll die trying for command.
What am I now? A chess piece on a flat glass floor, breaking beneath
my feet. A note in a bottle uncorked, unread,

unless you'll rip the tubes out, breathe on your own, before
I leave to turn back one last time.
Please call out to me. Say something, Tell me who I am now.
Even Lot's wife must have had a name before
they called her Salt.

Japanese Cats

In Haiku there is one rule: no cats.
They are too cute, too easy to win our love.
That is the rule.
Today
my cat saw the blossoms blow
and begged
to go outside,
but first he turned to sniff his food
one last time.

This is not a haiku for
I have more I want to say:

I want to talk about my Beloved
who left before the dawn overlapped the sky—
how first he stopped to conjure one last sight
We entered it together in a bubble
floating toward a needle,

a second stolen
turning back
before the blossoms.

Stunned

I don't know about dropping a full bottle of wine on the pavement in Pisa
Or both leaving our hats in the locker room in Maryland on the same day
Or talking about our neighbor in West Virginia who killed his cat
As we stand hand in hand looking
At the milk of the moon shining on the whole world
I alive— you dead—saying if this could happen, anything could.

Navy Wife

1964

Among things lost was a golden rose hanging on a chain
given by a teacher before
my 5-year-old daughter had her tonsils out.
I vacuumed it up on the rug. I didn't know
how, then, to open the machine. The twins were 3 years old
drinking bottles, standing on the couch. I was
too pregnant to lean over, to find the chain.
I said we'd try to find another one. I promise,
but I'd have to leave her at the hospital, alone, overnight.

1970

My youngest daughter loved that new sweater, the one with angora animals.
She got it for Christmas, it was thrown in the wash
by accident, a gift from her Nana, tiny fuzzy creatures, shrunk beyond wearing.
So much was hurried. We tried to find one like it.

1944

The sweater was cut with scissors from my arm when I broke the bone.
Roosters knit on the wool, a figured sweater, the first of its kind,
such a generous grandmother to give such a present. I walked it in front
of a car. I was told to tell the insurance company
it was not my fault. The only sweater we found to replace it was
blue with white stars and that was 4 years later.

1950

The gold Bulova watch I wanted so much, waited for so long, I finally
got for high school graduation. What made me go running into the
ocean,
the next day, swimming, without taking it off.

1964

My husband lost his friends. He says he cannot count them,
he cannot see their faces. He cannot say their names.
He felt their presence, flying on his wing, protecting him. He cared so much.

1962

The crystal earring brought back from a war cruise
was thrown out with the purse.
The present bought on shore duty, a single day off the carrier,
a jewel still warm in my hand. The only one left.

Navy Wife, 2010

Once You Were Young With Soft Hands

Now showing your age. But once you flew
so high up you could not see the world

showing its grief like old wounds.
Bright light from the moon

made us look like a blue planet.
Night rose like dark water,

a knife edge across the desert in a sharp line.

No "up" or "down" but *toward* and *away* from earth,
the sun exploding energy at your back.

Now in your snowsuit plowing, there is a memory
of the sky stoking fires very far away.

Heart on a Leash, 1998

Haberdashery

I wish I hadn't made fun of him that day at Union Station when he walked away from the tie rack with the same green and blue striped tie he had in his closet at home. Green and blue slanted stripes. "You have one," I laughed. He said *maybe the stripes are wider on the other one.* I proved I was right. They were identical. I proved it. "Why have two exactly alike?" *Because I like that tie,* he said. *I always liked this tie.* Then I recalled when I was 17, and his mother took the hat right off my head. She liked it. Actually my father did this when she said *Isn't that adorable.* He took it right off my head and handed it to her. I never found another. None of this is what I want to talk about. This second, I want to show you the way the sun lights up the tree, such a funny slice of light, it couldn't be made by design, the way it hits the angle of green. There will never be another one like it.

Supreme Rushing*

*(*acupuncture point)*

Do you know what I can't do?
I can't stop crying,
You know what I can do?
I can stand on one stone
and touch the other
without bending my knee,
I walk down the hill
carrying a large oak leaf,

There is sun on all sides,
I pass the piano teacher's
fine white house with
its buried place of dreams
which remembers names
better than I do.

In the music of the past
will be a place
by the water where once
I found my husband
and children who were real

Poems, New and Selected, 1993

Foot Above Tears*

(*acupuncture point)

The small group by the pool,
the water almost clear of clouds,
the small group which came together.

Most of all,
it will be the sweet man
with the white hair
I'll miss the most.

The year dropped down around us
like a pillow
stained blue with tears.

Going to the empty shelves
I brought back all the cans,
putting them where they were,
even the half-finished cat tuna
and the jar with tomatoes still clinging.

Although the children are married maybe
I could bring them back to their rooms
for just the day,
or I could find an old friend
still by the beach in California

where I've never been
but remember fondly.
I'd know her by the bando
in her hair, her small white gloves.

My happiness will go on without you
as yours will without me,
oh sure we would rather have loved than not
but the habitual order of things
kept us in our place until
we passed through each other and
we'll never quite recover from that.

Poems, New and Selected, 1993

Dear Ken in an Orange Sweater

Do you remember the trip we took north through Newark
stopping by the river
the soot and alleys of New York
just a stone's throw away
on the large rocks looking out at the moving water
when Summer was prettier,
before the dispiriting war,
sitting in the sun warming to a brilliant future,
the slope was rocky and yet we found a way
through the fence to get closer,
this was before the birds called about the storm,
you let me wear your orange sweater
when the wind came up,
we talked about
how far it must be between stars here at night.

But who am I now that I should want this back,
this would be before engagement and marriage,
before children's fingerprints on the pantry door,
before you held my bread over the open flame
on the stove in Italy because
we didn't have a toaster,
I felt the orange sweater wrapped on my shoulders
until I gave it back and got into the car

to head south or did we go north from there.
I don't need the sweater for what is the use of comfort
in memory, that would be 60 years before your hands
started trembling whenever you lifted a glass,

I look at photos we took
and console myself saying *where are you Ken* but
where is anyone when we don't see them in the room.
I wish the scraggy flowers growing there by
the river turning to weeds would stop blooming
so they could catch up with death,
all this on our way to someplace else to see the sights,
you smiling in your sweater is what I'll see
in the moment between here and there
when I turn toward the orange light.

Key West

A button falls off
Hold the break between your fingers

Then sew it on
The web of time expands

Wipe away the last crumb on the counter

With a flat hand
Among the yellow flowers is survival on a stalk

Is a wish on the Winter moon
More to come in the morning

Someone is playing the piano upstairs
The wisdom of certainty without pain

Warm in February

This Sounds Like Something I Would Say, 2010

Inflamed Like Trumpets

The argument was more than that. You loved me bright
then perfect heat fell in my eyes.
Whatever stayed was just an angel from Hell.
It will leave at last, dripping softly,
but oh the plunging
the overhang.
All transparencies across the life we've lived
were total stars turning into yellow tides.
I'm accustomed to these springs
but the pain waits and waits to privilege us.

Cuffed Frays, 2001

Fixation

Every day I go to the Naval Academy pool where Ken and I swam
together
And I plunge under the water and pretend Ken's in the lane next to me
And I know he moves two laps for every one of mine
And I pretend we're in the Key West pool and he's in the next lane
Where it is shining ribbons off the bottom
And I'll get out first and go along the white stone path
Through the hibiscus past palms by the water
Into the shower room where I always slip on the floor
Then I'll be waiting for him outside at the picnic table watching the scuba
divers
And he'll come out and we'll wonder where to eat lunch maybe go into
town
For conch soup but I have writing to do and he needs to rest after such a
workout
But whatever happens we need to be up at 6:12 because tonight
That's sunset time and everyone claps on the pier and we're never late
With a martini for him and a tequila for me in plastic cups
Then a sound breaks my trance and I realize that it's coming from my
own throat
Like the clacking the cat makes when watching the birds outside
It's caught like a squeal under water a squeezed sob and I climb out
And I rush past midshipmen who're laughing and telling their jokes and
complaints
And I take a fast shower with the sound still coming from the back of my
throat
Hoping no one has heard me as I dress and move out fast already planning when I can
Return.

30

Messages from the Other World

These are not on the road to nowhere. Just when I can't take anymore up
come the dead. How they do it I
don't know, with all their strengths and depths. They play music on the
radio like Juliette Greco, from
years ago, our favorite singer. These are not memorized memories—your
sock caught in the sleeve of my
sweater from an old laundry— quarters shining in the grass in the back-
yard although fenced and gated—
lights going on and off. I agree I'd put everyone's mind at ease to call it
coincidence, or parallels to life
from undercurrents of thought, but did I tell you that tonight I put the last
log in the fireplace—although
it's well into Spring— and without a match, I returned and it was already
alive with flames?

July

It's 10:10 and my program goes on at 11pm and here I am carrying my recording tape to the station
although it's so far from home into DC with all our dirty sheets in my arms but maybe I can wash them
there except for the coins in the glass of water all those slippery dimes unless the manager's there at his
desk so I can't launder in front of him but everyone is nice and wants to chat it's been so long since I've
been on the air at the station again and the tape I thought was Frederick Douglass is actually Obama thank
God it's a good one everyone laughing and crying at the cherry joke how he cut down the tree so it must
be a good one and although the rich poet drops by to say she met another rich poet in the airport I cannot
wait because your white bathrobe is at the cleaners thank god it only cost a dime to pick up although a
wet one and I have to stumble home through the fields where some idiot let loose a bag of mice to aerate
the soil so I have to watch where I walk around over and through and this is just one day without you.

Pity the Poor Cat Who Mourns

I am tired of your crying, caring for your own comfort.
Self compassion was never meant for animals
and yet you try
pushing your pile of papers as if it were a blanket,
making the familiar *strange,*
like artists do, to manage grief.
You have to know someone before you can forget him, and
what, tell me, did you know —
only that he is dead —
and worse, that but he's no longer young.
Too much to think about. Two in one.
I see confusion feasts upon your heart and how you wake up with a start:
Dreaming of Las Vegas? Where no birds live? What a howl of loss
you give — and who could blame you.
Now you roll in a pastiche of sand pissing in full view,
your clawing and moaning uncluttered by morality
walking out your jungle box veiled in dust.
Listen — you have no uplifting memories of the world with him,
so how can you fake grief, or is it emptiness disguised as hunger
that makes you eat and eat.
It has been one month now that we were left alone.
Each night the light goes on and off and on until
you push it from off the table, and I don't blame you.
The spirit world does not
interest me either as it knows nothing of our mourning.

How I wish I could curl up like you
into a ball of fur, purring with belief that
he'd come upstairs at any moment. Surely this is what you think and why
not—
you didn't see the machine he was hooked to before his death,
tubes with lights blinking on and off until his body begged itself free.
How can you help but believe— if you wait long enough—
he'll fill your bowl again and pick you up to hold.
Poor dumb creature, foolish and confused, how I pity you,
for soon you'll find for certain, in spite of your best fears,
I am all that you have left.

They Live Where Death Ever Reaches

There will be someone there waiting.
You will wear the gray silk suit
before it gets ruined in the rain
on North Capitol Street.
You will find a love and are allowed to keep it.
It is news sliding into light.

We are lying in beds watching
the sunset and talking about how
long we've known each other
and all the homes we lived in.

The old pain in the chest comes
over me and I can't breathe
knowing one of us will leave
the other first and then
I try not to think about it,

instead think of tomorrow when there's
hot tea in bed with the sunrise and a
crispy bagel from the oven – just
us two together growing older,
and never dying, the thought
of it keeping me alive.

Heart On A Leash, 1998

Wedding Day

Birds sweeping past the graveyard sing notyetnotyet
   call me to cross the water through a gate into the garden.

The white doorknob turned slightly. The chair moved
   to seat me. My hand near the fire was to

learn the way of it. Days stared at my face.
   All things which could go wrong were

my wedding guests. Before carrying the candle
   through the marsh, before following the casket,

there'd be this dance, the one with yellow leaves.
   I looked about and saw my future in

the paintings on the wall, a boat taking the water,
   a bride coming home on foot, a game about to ring

with diamonds. I felt as large as life in that
   door of the church. What would you have done?

People presented luxuries, the rugs, the cake.
   I turned away my tears, which would be louder than bells

chiming across the lake, softer than piano music.
   What I had in mind was a picnic on the bank,

sleeping on the blankets before that high-pitched sound
   signaled of our danger. We left before the snow.

Holding my white glove, running through the fields of
   grain, stumbling into a prairie of flowers, falling into their song,

we searched for the perfect banquet on a plate.
   Everywhere, we tried and failed, but we may have found it.

Cuffed Frays, 1991

Please Accept My Donation

For Ken

I want to thank you for dazzling heaving deserts praising love,
for extravagant birds and clowns.
Please forgive the calamitous leaping over sand, the shouts of fire,
the startling rings. I didn't know.
Oh sure there were springs exiled, new pipes, other conceptions –
We're only human. Child, girl, man: What's the difference?
Afternoons hasten. That's why I want to say, most of all,
I memorized your paper gardens, drifting stones, the willow trees.
I'll always remember the sun we survived, the vulnerable surfs, waking.
I deeply appreciate the way we addressed each other faithfully,
powdered gold faces, crossing like this, tomorrow in mirrors.
It was all a lovely motion of fleece, feathers on the sea

Cuffed Frays, 1991

Didn't We Have Fun

Key West with its bright yellow rental car
The lobby in Easton with orange slices floating in cold water
Steamed clams in New York City, 12 blocks away
Navy reunions with young wives with blonde hair
Tennis, your strong serve
Olives beside my Mimosa to make up for your Martini
Morning prayers
My looking over my shoulder, watching, saying No
The new vacuum cleaner
Breakfast, lunch, and dinner
Your handwriting in the checkbook
Celtic music while you sketched
The cat on your newspaper
Italy's sunflowers turning toward us
Your kiss on our girls' foreheads
Goodbye to all that
And to your lungs filling up
And Goodbye to your hand on mine saying
Don't Worry I'll Get You There.

Thoughtforms

After getting off the bus
the man with the sports page
woke the beggar lady up,
on her corner,
to give her a dollar bill,
without her asking,
I told my husband.
"That's what giving is"
he answered.

Trenton, 1990

Consumer Report

I thought about it a long time because I ran out of staples so I tiptoed down to his office. I didn't know what else to do. Next it was the typing paper neatly stacked beside the desk. Thank God he thought ahead with batteries in the drawer for my mouse and keyboard. I used to play office once when I was very young. I'd walk around the street and write down all the numbers that I saw on tiny squares of paper, put in shoe boxes stacked inside the closet wall. But this cannot go on. How long. Today my swimming goggles broke. I know he has two pairs brand new inside his swimming bag. I cannot bear to open it. They are my style, bought the same day as my own. His swim bag zipper is closed all the way. I'll wear the old ones another day. It's always the same, these seasons that come and go, I steal what I can from him. Shoplifting from the life I loved is no way to live. What will I do when the Azaleas stop blooming ?
I stole his bottle of orange- flavored gin. What will I do when we run out of supplies?

The Magellanic Clouds of Vietnam

How far we travelled, sweetheart...
Stephen Spender

When you came home from
the minutes of war
sick from passion and duty

you lived
in the past

and the future

anywhere but here.

You walked in
suspicious

of desires and
other rites of loss.

"Promise me you'll
only dream
dreams of me," I'd said

but that spoke to a life
where death
had not yet reached

and a time
smaller
than your experience.

It took eleven years of walking
for you to reach
the marble names
afraid you'd find yours on the list
and afraid you wouldn't.

Fated to be alive
when your friends were dead,

you smoothed
your mournful clothes

and turned toward the Memorial.

I found Buzz Eidsmoe's name
you called. This is why I was
afraid to come
afraid to see it.
It's here. I see it.
I can remember their faces
But not all their names.

You talked about perspectives,
the marble of memorial,

the angles
simple
unadorned

contained by a sun

shining on black surfaces

surprisingly radiant.

But You Forgot to Say Goodnight

"I see the light on the mountain"
You said, your last words.
"Tomorrow I'm going home
And mat that new painting
And start my bas relief of
Chuck Klusmann escaping from
The POW camp, show how he got
Through the barbed wire, leaving
All that pain, imagine the jungle
But he was finally free to go
Not knowing
What came next, but not caged in."

Wife

When we were young and estranged
we met in the hall. He pressed
me against his uniform, my
satin blouse, we fell to the
floor in love—no we did not—
we stood— I wore my chiffon
blouse, distant in the kitchen—
or we walked in the park—no—
it was our wish that we
fell to the floor in a way
like never before but—no—
it must have been some other selves
who should have worn those clothes.
Now he is sailing away.

Navy Wife, 2010

Ken Is Alive Each Night

This time we're staying with another Navy couple
Such a small ragged house
But these are our circumstances—
No tragedy, hunger, or orphans in the Navy
Just the humility of small cardboard kitchens
The bitterness of temporary quarters—
Children are riding tricycles in the cramped bedroom
But how kind they were to take us in for a brief stay—
One child has a fever and the rusting clock says time to go—
It is sweet to be with my husband again
Even in someone else's house—
We regret leaving—
our arms spilling with clothes—
Empty hangers falling to the floor—
There is so much to carry, the suitcase is full, we move to the car
Not knowing if I will have another dream —
Not knowing where we can possibly go next.

Can I Count on You

If I were lying in a boat in a wedding gown would you see me
floating by
If I named a star after you would you lie in the grass looking up
If I lived in a white house would you come sit on my front porch
If I were caught in a bad dream would you please wake me up
If I had a plaid blouse would you help me button it
If I could jitterbug would you do the double dip
If I were a red cardinal would you hold out a sunflower seed
If I caught all the fireflies in the world would you give me a big jar
If the night nurse forgets to come would you bring me a glass of
water
If I have only minutes to look at the silky moon will you come get
me

A Day at the Fair

Because I missed you so much
I entered the contest.
It was easy.
The only requirement was that I cut a heart
out of the center of my head.
It would grow back.
Even if our teeth touched when we kissed
other contestants
we'd get a chance for second prize.
I couldn't wait.
Besides, who doesn't like a picnic—
The Chinese man was playing a violin. All
our words were kites flying in the wind.
It's O.K. I assured the woman next to me
They're all arbitrary anyway
and they don't always mean what they say.
She borrowed my main ingredient
in gratitude.
I didn't care,
because each man there was to choose
the woman he wanted to feed him a cherry
on a silver spoon.
One man stuck his thumb in the spoon
and popped it right in his mouth before the start.

That's why he lost the contest.
But before I could enter the pain
of the lesson learned,
you were there in the chair on the stand by the band,
with the back of your neck just right,
ready for kissing,
and a doll with paper wings won, just for me,
in your hands.

Trenton, 1990

Going through the Files

I wish I didn't open that one of the seed catalogue that said Hoorah For
Summer. I want you to know, Ken, I'm still psychic for what it's worth.
I saw Angel holding a brown black cat in her arms and when I told her
boys they said Yes! There is one that comes around all the time. Angel
didn't believe me at first as she thought she'd sent a photo but she hadn't.
I don't know why it matters but I like having a special gift, a look in-
side the world which tells me that time and distance are just circles of
thought we are closed in— and then when the Forsythias die out front,
which they're almost starting to do, I won't have to say Oh No, OH NO.
Although even now I can't look at them as beautiful as they are because I
know what's coming.

If in Fact He Ever Lived

I see his red and white striped shirt hanging against all the others left
untouched by his breath. I say *Thank You* to that shirt for all the poetry
readings and places, and also to the Navy Dress White for Angel's wed-
ding. I say *Thank you* to each one, following them down the rack talking
to a closet. Perhaps he wanted freedom from all these but I am still in the
forest and wonder about the meals we've forgotten and the peaches once
eaten—did they exist? That sounds like some soul-seeking philosophy.
No. It is the quick cold snow of truth, biting and cold, gone as snow.

The Man Who Got Away

Why you accepted their death plan, I'll never know. I guess you were getting ready to die again so you put on your best pink shirt and took the death pill in your hand. I of course went along riding shotgun with you into the dark. How unafraid you were I still can't understand, and I, sobbing uncontrollably, still holding your hand. We had one hour before your end and how do you suppose I felt when the young swimmer we used to know met up with us and you forgot to die, and all the pills in the world could not take away that last energy, you jumped in the air beyond any death decree right there in front of me. Once she worked in a kitchen store and gave you a large steel sieve. She had only one tear on her cheek for your life and I had all those years. She had a moment. I own your death. And I have the steel sieve.

The Man in the Machine

15 days now you are attached to tubes that breathe, head back
while in my dream I wear the satin dress
you bought me
broken now in back and fixed
with three shining safety pins that gleam
blood pressure perfect, heart perfect, lungs failing.
I can hold my dress together with one hand
or take it off
wearing my old tee shirt beneath
to ride on back your breathing machine now fit with wheels,
without my shoes—
I left them with you
last night when your machine took off
changing to a giant ship sailing out of sight.
STOP I shout. My shoes are there and so
you came floating back,
one eye open, saying you *want out.*
Now both eyes closed again—
Why did I leave that day you failed—when you said the sun
was much too bright—
I said *close your eyes and make it dark.*
The last words that you heard from me,
Close your eyes I said *and make it dark.*
How you lurched one moment when they stopped the Drip,

your wrists trapped and tied to bed rails by two ropes.

How you reared and tore and yanked,

thinking you were a prisoner of war once again

behind the enemy lines.

The doctor says, *this is just as hard on us*. Oh yes?

Then he purrs you back into what they call *euphoria*.

Oh that is not euphoria, my poor doctors. I know euphoria—

It looks like a race car he's driving at Lime Rock,

a motorcycle across country to Michigan,

a safe landing on an aircraft carrier in the pitch black of night—

It looks like a zipper on my wedding gown

before it broke in half—

Yes this machine will win for sure,

and you, my man inside, you'll lose –how many times

have I sat by to watch you win,

a champion, top ten, All American.

Should I bring this machine home among your trophies from

this last big race you've lost.

Shall I keep it with your swimming medal—

with mementos, from the past—

We cannot win them all, you've said—

but we need something from this final cut

before the big event—of losing—

Losing is a keepsake to remember.

If we give up loss, what will we have left.

The Day They Gave Husband Away

The curtains are blowing the trees through
                  the roof
The chill comes through the room
         pushing the curtains aside
People are hugging outside laughing
        asking for a ride
They don't know someone is dying
The curtains are red, the color of blood
        blood lost from the
body's thirst
From the wind comes a note from the sound of his throat
F minor blowing the curtains
               the color of blood
There are pills on the floor
The door knob breaks off
The fan blows the curtains sharply between them
She twists her hair
             She rushes to find him
but the curtain has dropped sharply between them
           Perhaps she will see him
on a Monday across the street in the rain
      or riding by in a cab
           or on a Tuesday.

The Embroidered Pillow

Even after all those stitches I made
with such care and diligence, day after day
--the red ones for Viet Nam
--the crisscross blue for the seas between us
--the swirls of yellow for brick roads we traveled
--the spears of green for so many Springs—
Even after all that—
you held my arm so I couldn't move to enter
the contest.
I wanted to win so much.
You said *Let the young girls have it. It's*
their time now, and I said, "But look at all the days
I've spent threading needles,
my fingers raw from working them,
the piercing of steel into cloth over and over."
You put your arms around me even though
I tried to get away, but my hand caught
In the curve of your sleeve and I couldn't pull it free.
Stand here on the terrace with me, you said, *and look*
at all we've done.
"But those beautiful colors no one will ever see!" I cried.
You led me in and said, *Come now with me.*
There's nothing left for us to do. Put the pillow down.
Let's rest our heads on it, together, it's getting late.

Tide Flow E66

I was afraid you'd dash off like a hero and not look back
      You'd die with the sinew of something left unsaid
I was afraid I'd cry at Jiffy Lube
I was afraid of your empty shirts hanging from the spine of their hangers
      Or that I'd move the quiver of truth the way I wanted
I was afraid of losing my balance, a broken sparrow at the stairs
      I saw the edge of your shadow from the corner of my eye
I was afraid of the space after "What else do I have to do, but be with you?"
      I was afraid I'd forget how you looked
I was afraid of the first car crash, broken tools, my first flat tire
I was afraid to see you put into your final cement home
          Now, I'm not afraid of anything.

Warmth

Last night it was a new
Cardigan you wanted in a
Handsome knit Scottish weave
$1,080.The amount of my Social
Security and how blue
You were that I demurred
But you can have it now and
Even more—you tried
To buy me several wools
To make up for
Your buying yours
But I need nothing now and
I have no wish to go in stores
Or have what would be mine
Or even buy you yours
My dear dead man so
Unfashionable and cold
Don't you know we are each
Beyond heat and sweater poor.

Crystal Radio

The little boys are playing in the workshop.
The monologue is of screwdrivers
and broken radios. They lean over
wires, untying commandments of mystery.
The plain boxes, disassembled,
as a grandfather pulls apart all
colors. Love makes no sound
while Newton's
laws of motion are at work,
speeding between the tongue and the mind,
they speak. They make motion from parts.
They create what I have never written.
They don't know this can't go on without them.
They don't know what a memory is worth.
It is a sight to command, the
old man leaning over, the boys in a dream
of their own making. He is saying
"I'm not done with you yet."
They are thinking this will go on forever.

Sounds Like Something I Would Say, 2010

The Art of Discard

Said The Sculptor to the Writer:

"Somebody wants what you're writing but nobody cares if I sit hour after hour dripping molten bronze on hot steel. I don't care. It's the watching I want, the way I hold my hand so still. If I wait too long the metal will melt— If I move too quickly the bronze will harden. I live for this. The watching. The moment to touch bronze to steel, the second to pull it back All you need is a pencil. I have leather, masks, rods, machines, sanders, polishers, fire. You can hide your rejects in a drawer. Mine stand in front of me, larger than I am, gleaming and incomplete. What do you have faith in?" he asked me. "I have faith in failure," he said, "then making it beautiful, something that will last."

This Sounds like Something I Would Say

What I did, when Ken stood up, in that movie
theater, was *swallow.*
I held the saliva in my mouth two hours
all through the movie "Ivy."
I didn't dare swallow, because the body,
should not make noise at that age.
Later, he would swear he never heard me gulp.
That day, at age thirteen, love was
given to me.
Today, clouds look like they did,
small bunches, white puffs, behind branches.
Today, on a day just like this, Jan and I would walk down the
hill.
Jan is with me in kindergarten and everything smells like
Bread.
We are sitting together on small chairs at the Hermitage
Library.
That was before we knew what Eve really did. Even then we
wondered about the stories, the room we were in: Did the
light make the path to the door?
Or did the path make the light? There was no one to ask
about bright windows, shadows, or what Eve would do
or what she actually did
and what was already widening within us.

This Sounds Like Something I Would Say, 2010

Pulled along by the Moon

The asparagus is growing to the sky indifferent to earth
A letter to nowhere
The squirrel delivers a leaf to my husband in thanks for past meals
No one is here
Do you remember the time the wisteria grew inside the back door
It had to be cut
And now the Azalea is back with a chorus of fire with a hummingbird
Romancing the feeder
In the pastures of Heaven we are told there is no sorrow — that even in
this
Sandstorm there's something to praise
I am told we should thank Winter for all this — something like thanking
Death for his life.

Most Things Don't Have Conclusions

Everything fit nicely
      The opulence of that store
The gowns we ordered came in
      white chiffon with appliques
         at the hem
The white satin shoes with embossed flowers
But Mother   I can't wear
      high heels
I am old   I can wear flat shoes
and the hem will sweep across the floor
How will we arrange it to travel
The Angel of Death appears
         He is so handsome
         in his Frank Sinatra hat
He looks up my husband's phone number
         from my notebook
so I know I must call in the morning   I meant to   I hope it's not
         too late
All the beautiful arms of his sculpture reach out in a filigree of
light

I always wanted his happiness to depend on me
      Now what do I pray for.

Learning from Buddha

The cat likes to lick
a piece of butter
at the end of a knife
propped up by the window
so he can watch the birds
today I forgot the butter and the knife
he didn't care
he knows
some days
there are no birds.

Past, Present, Future

From here, we could almost see the road.

Some days we could see it from the window –
the woods, the far hill –
but what with rain and snow
blocking the view
and our fear of the space
between us
we could think of travel.

At times we tried to leave
and that's when we held each other
close in our arms
naming over and over the words
mouth, eye, tongue, heart
in hopes we'd understand
the fear we felt,
its origin still deep in the body.

For a time the chill
was heavy,
years absent of fire and rapture
but at the blizzard's end,
a madness was dissolved, leaving
only its tiny slivers of light.

That night a flight of stars
told of a trust beyond the senses
imagined without memory or mind,

where showers would rinse the last
issues of ice from our eyes.

A new sun cut across the line of trees
maintained in silence, yet
saying more than ever before.

Then we heard it from the meadows,
a flashing of music –
with its own path through the branches
turning everything to a movement of green
coming out of the air like time
          to greet us.

Trenton, 1990

Florida

Scarred though we are
by what we've left,
will we remember it less
without children,
our car packed full with hope.

We move toward a place with
no poets
but there never were
more than
good people who pulled
praise from our curses
while we sat stupid and crying
that we were still alive.

I have finally let go
of something I never had,
finding the miracle
in forgiving,
that there is nothing to forgive.

Now only time is left to greet us,
the life and death parts,
never tidy

but nicely inclusive.
Then off we go again with the
starting up of it,
our nails ribbed with age and
its inevitability.

Should we excuse others
for all we've done to them–
before giving in
to the vanishing dark,
the feeling no language can speak,
the open air of our own music,
the sound of the rain on the wall.

Poems, New and Selected, 1993

Heart Correspondence*

(*acupuncture point)

I take the tea,
we place the cups
side by side,
the handles are turned
mine is on the right,
you put your honey in
I stir it
I say *is there enough*
you add more, a little milk
no cream, I say *more honey*
you stir it
I stir it again
absentmindedly, like living
twice with this love
which has no need for memory.

Poems, New and Selected, 1993

The Perfect Day

There was one moment when
the house floated among the trees
of Summer, maybe three o'clock,
when everything was warm
and smelled of powder, when
our mothers were in the kitchen
and it was perfectly still.
The sun in the afternoon
was lace on the street as
I stood clean and warm in a
white starched sundress. I did
not know what to call that feeling
… one moment of balance…
when the air was the same exact
temperature as my blood, smooth
inside and out. This was before
dinner time where there would
be iced tea and sliced cold
tomatoes, and the sound of a spoon
against a quiet table.
I think of that now as you lie
beside me asleep, wrapped in
a comforter of red and white,
as I watch the white snow
from the window rising to its trees

to hide a woodpecker, red
and white and black.
I think how one moment cannot be
another, how the perfect day
is gone from us with its sweet
second of comfort and how this, too,
is almost gone, how soon I will
lie in another perfect moment and
remember your breathing in the silence
today as I watched the birds eating
the suet from the kindness of that
feeding. And, years later, again,
how I will wish for another moment,
wishing back to this moment, reaching
further to the perfect moment when
I stood alone by the street.

Poems, New and Selected, 1993

The Sun on the Cat

I've been walking the cat all day in my yard.
They say you can't harness a cat but I've leashed him
and he stays—
standing, walking, sniffing leaves.
Here there's no more waiting, no consequences,
no possibilities, no goodbye,
just warm rays on the animal that's left. And
I can't help but use this time
as meditation because it's hard figuring out
how people become
more like each other over the years.

The TV says *Tell Someone Who Cares*,
so instead I stay outside.
Should I disguise myself to avoid the neighbors?
Should I talk about the empty chair
to get their love?
The holy book said *where your life leads you, you must go.*
Oscar Wilde would say
'that shows signs of the trivial'—
Instead, describe it this way:
I'm suddenly in a beauty contest
in a foreign country where I cannot sing or dance,
and I'm 80 years old,

I only wanted to immerse in the culture
with everyone else
and no one is clapping!
But at least they're not laughing.

Forgiveness is found in memory.
What else could memory possibly be for?
I forgive myself for all the times
I could have held his hands
instead of other people's.

At first sight, we said nothing. After all,
I was only 13 years old.
The timeline was pretty good after that,
going steady at 15,
at 18, his mother's old diamond ring,
then, at 20 years, our marriage, walking 12 blocks
in NYC to find steamed clams.
It was the morality of the times to not sleep together
until we were married.
But the long life span would allow
an amity of trust.

Since "death" is still forming —we never
get tired of the pain in that character—
I am still in its patina and I know
I cannot speak for everyone
especially now, about marriage:
what defines the conception, the honesty,
the humility, risks,
what paradoxes made it better.

There were women who tried
their willful passion. One lost my
gold sequined purse, at first he didn't care,
but then he went out and bought me another
and another, although I already
had enough.

Like a day that was never ending,
the wounds of love taught us
the courage in ourselves for our arts,
a happiness of language that
never let us down—a camouflage
for our failures –the confidence of life
with some design—
saying hello to our souls.

The Christmas tree was not lighted this year.
The emergency room was lighted.
I was going home to get his glasses.
He thought he could finally read.
The cat knocked the tree over.
I should light it, it's not too late.
How many veils must we go through
while he is still in this world.

God said "I will shield you from fire."
Blood pressure, perfect. The nurse said.
She chose ICU because
she wanted to make a difference.
White count up.
Heart perfect.
Lungs failing.

My heart is raw as a root left out of the ground,
a radish, cold as the cellar it comes from.
Then she left me alone with him.

The bridge we stood on outside Trenton High
is now a golden bridge where we still stand.
Even then he was afraid to speak to me,
but he had thoughts worth thinking then
and he does still
even within the monastery of his machine.

I know it would be best to write something sassy
like Harry Shapiro's 'pastrami starting the world'
but I am not walking on 4th Street,
or by the Hudson River, like he was.
I'm in a hospital room in Annapolis, Maryland,
with a nurse I just handed chocolate chip brownies
to thank her.

What if I stood with one foot on the
railing and another extended over the
ocean with a black umbrella
over my head, would you
trust me to plan a funeral?
AT 17 years old he said "Don't leave me."
He said "Don't leave me" before they put the tube
in him.

Then I left —
to go to the bank where the teller was telling
and back where the nurses were nursing,
People, every one of them

assembling their various points of view.
It was OK to leave him for a moment
on the beach in 1953, where I whispered to him,
about the time
he brought home the first bikini
from a Navy cruise to France
and I stayed in the ocean six hours until the family
in the dunes finally went away, Today
I left him on the beach alone for a moment
in Boca Raton, Florida.

Last night his spirit left his body, it escaped,
while he lay breathing on the pump
and we went to a kooky bookstore
in D.C. How come we never found this one before?
The owner said I wrote her a letter
of recommendation to buy the store—
what fun meeting old students—
I left behind one of my sandals
and he went back and found it for me.
Oh the delicious books and food there,
we'll have to come back here more often.

If God answered every prayer, the nurse said,
no one would ever die.
When I adjusted the pillow,
he lifted one eyelid. It must have taken
enormous psychic strength.
I knew *WE MUST STOP THIS*.

January 15, 11:26 AM,
his 4 girls stood around his bed,

and one tear—we all saw it—
came from his left eye because
no one ever loved their daughters
more than he loved his.

The next day I found a scrap of page
torn from *The Daily Word* (Aug 31, 2012)
saying "I Have No Regrets."
It was under the rock from the Islands
on the window sill all this time.

Hello concrete world of the heart—

What did he know and when did he know it?
No use soul searching my intimate dreams,
reaching for heroes—
The death notice is free of charge in *The Post,*
because the reader wants a continuation
of a convention, and who could blame someone
at breakfast wakened to life by reading it.

I had said into the machine,
"Now you can finish the arms on the statue
you started, because on the astral plane
no torch is too heavy to lift.
Energy is a richer dimension," I said.

With the last shock of sun,
the sky is turning cold
and time to go inside, with these thoughts
like snow from the heart
going through my body.

The cat will stare out the window
to the frozen music of trees that say
turn back from the brink you came from.
I want to go back to raising the children
where the twins want to stay home from school
wearing red satin dresses,
and the others wear my mother-in-law's
old mink stoles—
where I feed them bread and butter for strength
and on the table would be a roast lamb
with candles around it for
when he'd come home.

Now I remember last night's dream.
After work
I took the bus to Ellsworth Avenue
where I grew up
but no one was home of course,
then to West Virginia
where the mail was stacking up,
thinking maybe I could get a hotel room
in DC for the night,
but then what of the next night?
Not particularly groundbreaking dreams,
I admit, although fear and pain were
melodic counterpoints—
as much as I've ever known—

the next thing I knew I was awake
The cat was driving me crazy. All
he wants to do is be held, knocking pictures

off the dresser, next the lamp he pushed off,
so I held him.
And I looked out and I saw
how good and true the dark is,
how it never lets us down, showing up again and again,
every single night,
how it is fair to everyone, rich and poor alike
and how much,
how very much it makes me love the sky.
Because it will always be there.

About the Author

Grace Cavalieri has written 17 books and chapbooks of poems, and 26 produced plays. Her most recent book of poems is *The Mandate of Heaven* (Bordighera Press.) She holds the 1993 & 2013 Allen Ginsberg Awards for poetry, the Pen Syndicated Fiction Award, the Bordighera Poetry Award, the Columbia Award, The Paterson Award, a CPB Silver Medal, among others. She was the 2013 recipient of the Association of Writers and Writing Programs George Garrett Award "for Outstanding Service in Literature." She founded and still produces "The Poet and the Poem," now recorded at the Library of Congress for public radio, celebrating 37 years on-air. She is poetry columnist/reviewer for *The Washington Independent Review of Books.*